I Am Thankful for...
Contemporary Cursive Handwriting Practice

This book has been designed to help children have fun as they practice writing the 26 cursive letters of the alphabet. Each activity features one of the letters, a Bible word containing the featured letter, a sentence relating to the Bible word, and a Bible verse. Not only do these activities help a child develop the skills and self-confidence that lead to success in writing, but they also foster discussions you can have with the child concerning the Bible verse and its relevance to the child's life.

How to Use This Book

- Establish a quiet, comfortable place in which you can work with the child.
- Plan a special time to work with the child. Create a warm, accepting atmosphere so the child will enjoy spending this time with you. Limit each session to one or two activities.
- Make sure the child understands the directions before beginning an activity.
- Discuss each page with the child. Give as much help and encouragement as necessary for the child to feel successful.
- Discuss each Bible verse with the child. See if he or she can relate it to his or her life.

© Grace Publications

I am
thankful for angels.

Aa

a a a

a a a

angels

Ann is an angel.

© Grace Publications   2   GP-75043 Contemporary Cursive Handwriting Practice

"...I am sending an angel ahead of you to guard you along the way..."

Exodus 23:20

I am
thankful for bread.

Bb

B B B

b b b

bread

Brother blessed the bread.

© Grace Publications   4   GP-75043 Contemporary Cursive Handwriting Practice

"Give us each day our daily bread."
Luke 11:3

I am
thankful for the cross. Cc

C C C

c c c

cross

Christ carried the cross.

© Grace Publications · 6 · GP-75043 Contemporary Cursive Handwriting Practice

May I never boast except in the cross of our Lord Jesus Christ…

Galatians 6:14

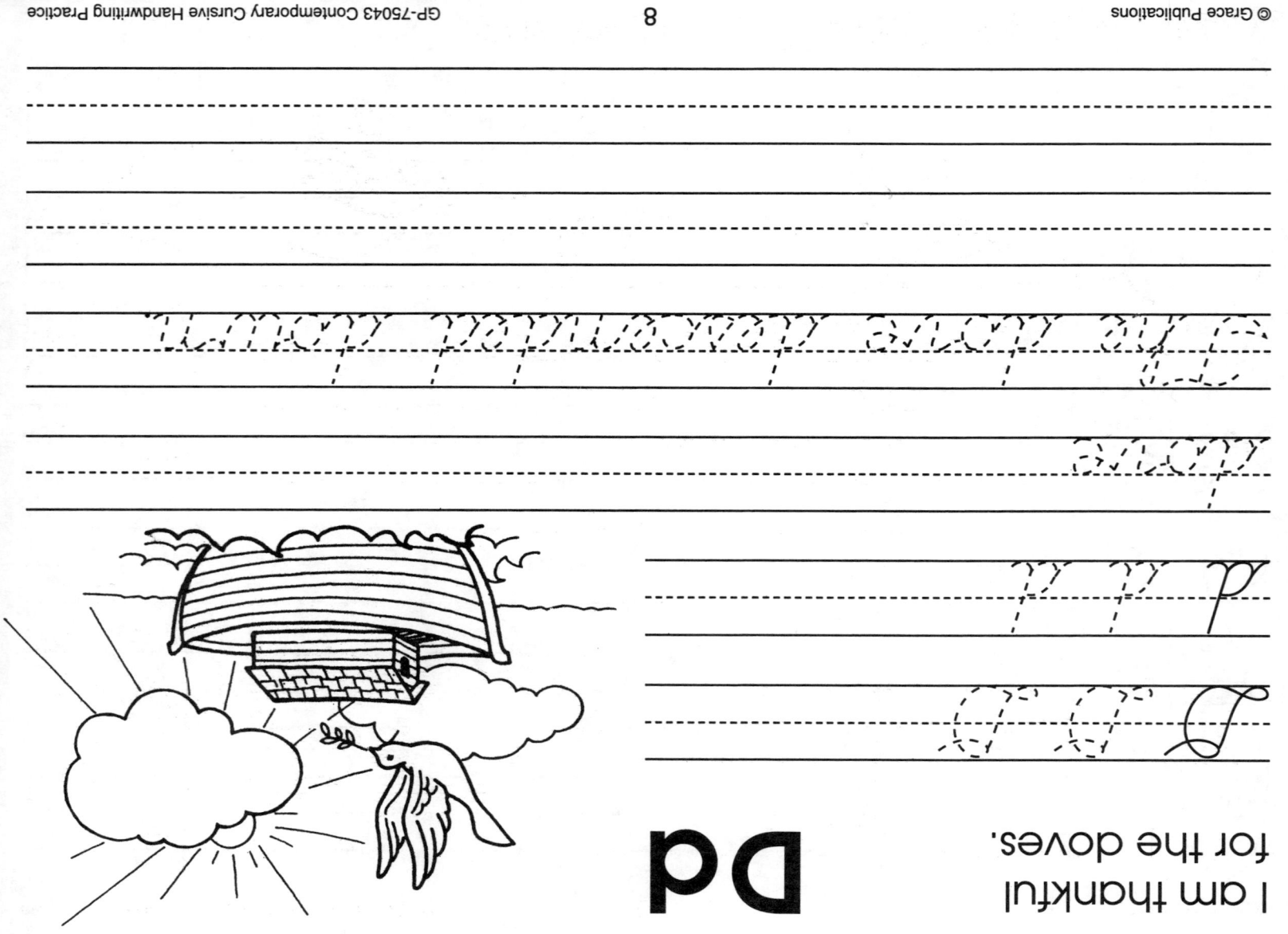

Dd

I am thankful for the doves.

...the Spirit descending on him like a dove.

Mark 1:10

I am thankful for the earth.

Ee

E e e

e e e

earth

Everyone embraces earth.

Let the heavens rejoice, let the earth be glad; ...
"The Lord reigns!"

1 Chronicles 16:31

I am thankful for fish.

Ff

F

f f f

fish

The fish fed 5,000.

© Grace Publications   GP-75043 Contemporary Cursive Handwriting Practice

Taking…the two fish and looking up to heaven, he gave thanks…

Matthew 14:19

I am thankful for God's grace.

Gg

grace

stay in God's grace.

© Grace Publications   14   GP-75043 Contemporary Cursive Handwriting Practice

...the gift of God's grace given me through the working of his power.

Ephesians 3:7

Hh

I am thankful for a happy heart.

Hh

Hh

happy

my hobby is art

Love the Lord your God with all your heart…

Deuteronomy 6:5

I am
thankful for Immanuel.

I i

I I I

i i i

Immanuel

The infant was Immanuel.

© Grace Publications

18

GP-75043 Contemporary Cursive Handwriting Practice

"...they will call him Immanuel"—which means, "God with us."

Matthew 1:23

I am
thankful for Jesus.

Jj

J J J

j j j

Jesus

Jesus joined John.

© Grace Publications

20

GP-75043 Contemporary Cursive Handwriting Practice

Then Jesus came…to the Jordan to be baptized by John.

Matthew 3:13

I am thankful for the
kingdom of heaven.

Kk

K K K

k k k

kingdom

God's kingdom is great.

© Grace Publications   22   GP-75043 Contemporary Cursive Handwriting Practice

"...the kingdom of God is within you."

Luke 17:21

Ll

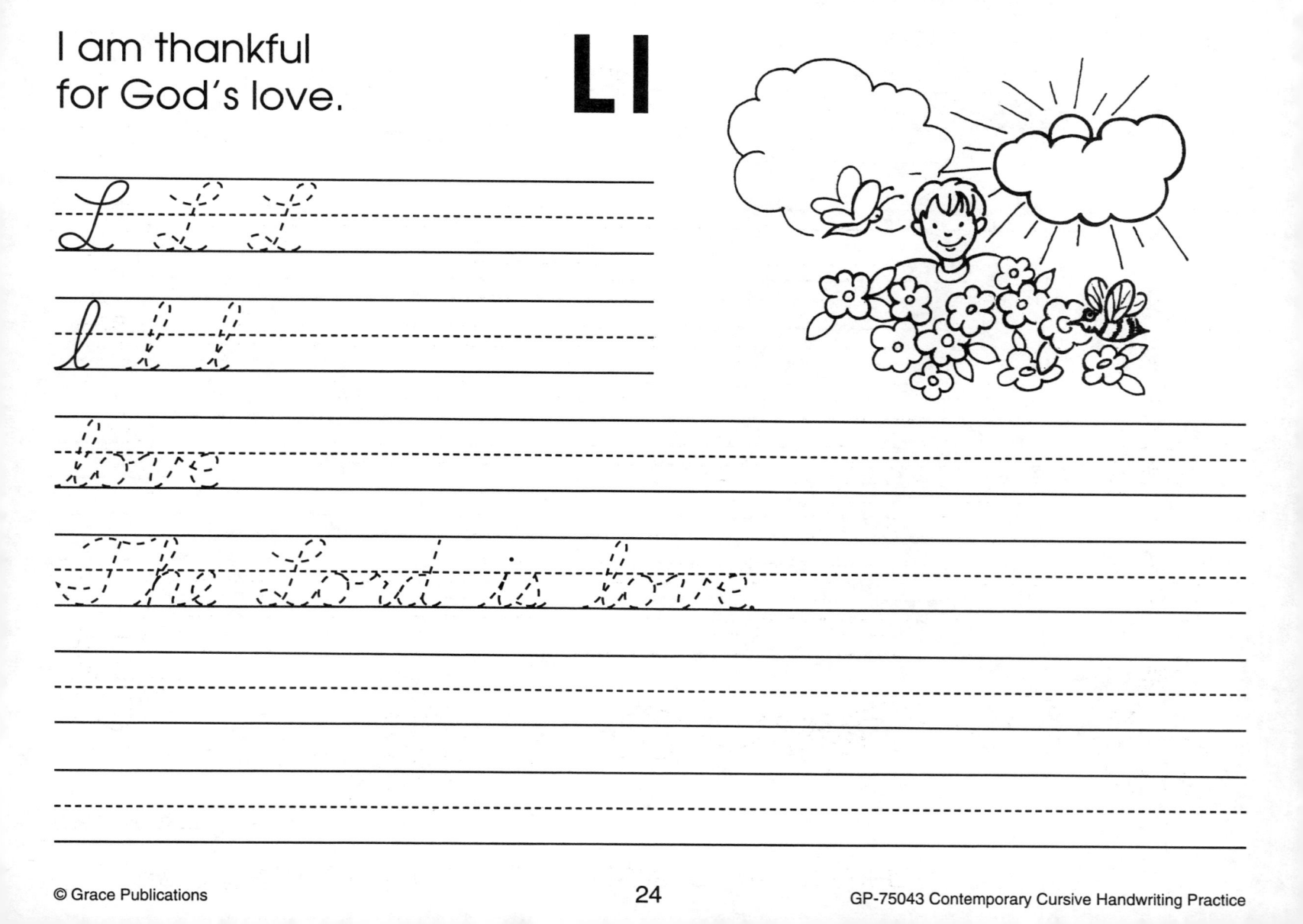

L L

l l

I love it very much.

I am thankful for God's love.

"...he is the faithful God, keeping his covenant of love..."

Deuteronomy 7:9

I am thankful for the Messiah. Mm

m m m

m m m

Messiah

The Messiah made miracles

© Grace Publications   26   GP-75043 Contemporary Cursive Handwriting Practice

"...The miracles I do in my Father's name speak for me."

John 10:25

I am thankful for my neighbor.

Nn

n n n

n n n

neighbor

Noah was a nice neighbor.

© Grace Publications

28

GP-75043 Contemporary Cursive Handwriting Practice

"...Love your neighbor as yourself."

Matthew 22:39

I am
thankful for offerings. **Oo**

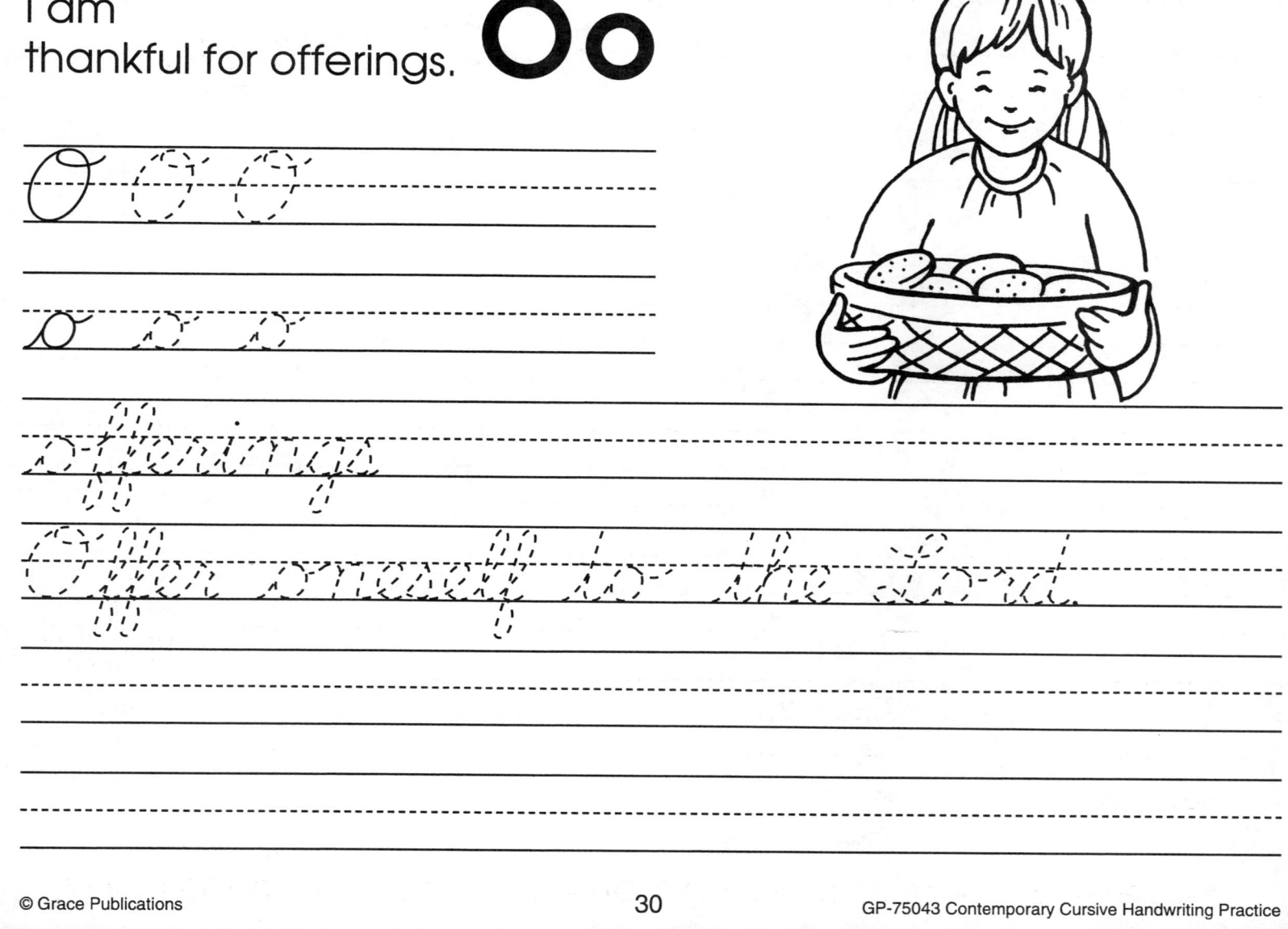

O O O

o o o

offerings

Offer praise to the Lord.

© Grace Publications
GP-75043 Contemporary Cursive Handwriting Practice

…Bring an offering and come before him; worship the Lord…

1 Chronicles 16:29

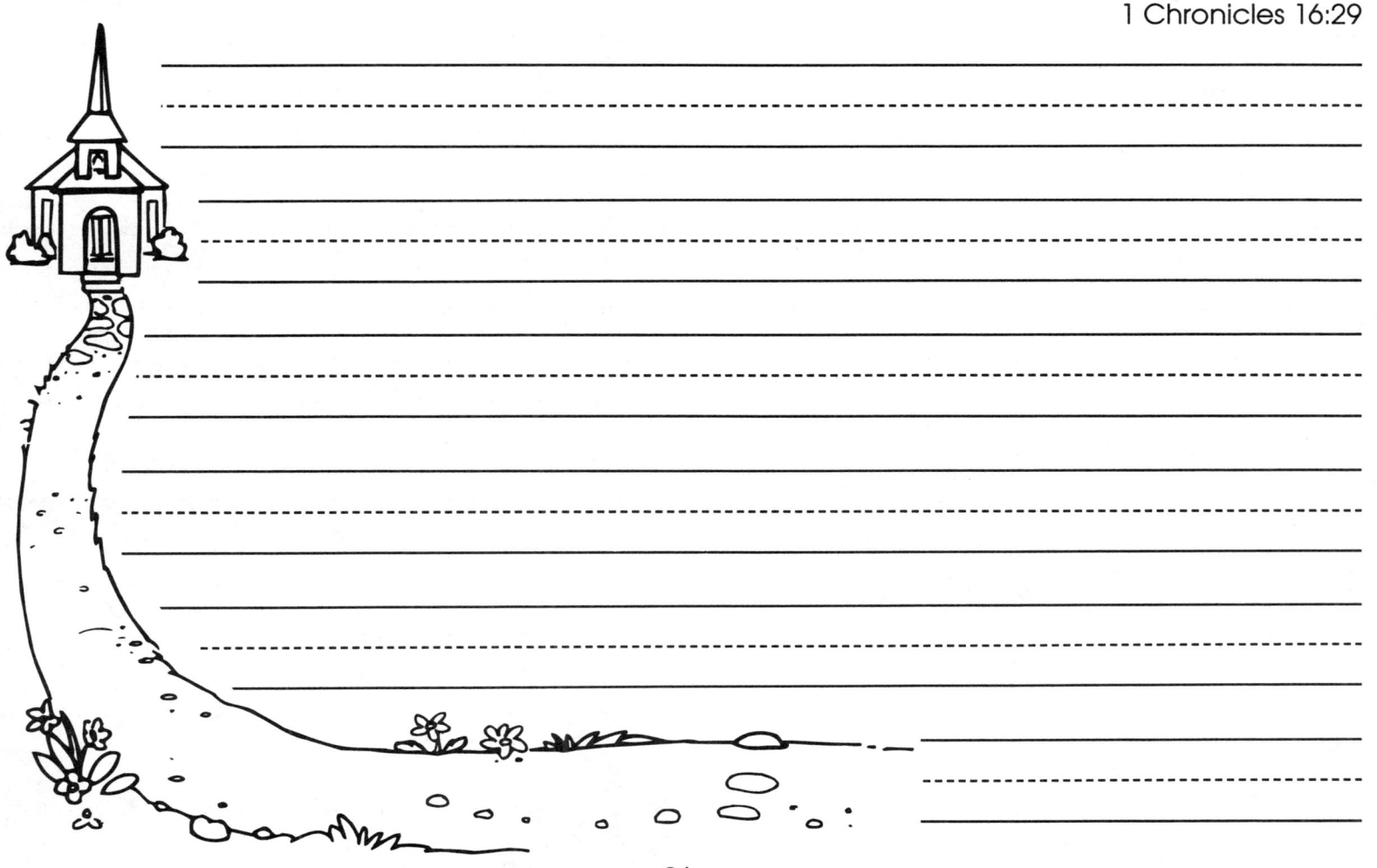

I am thankful for prayer.

Pp

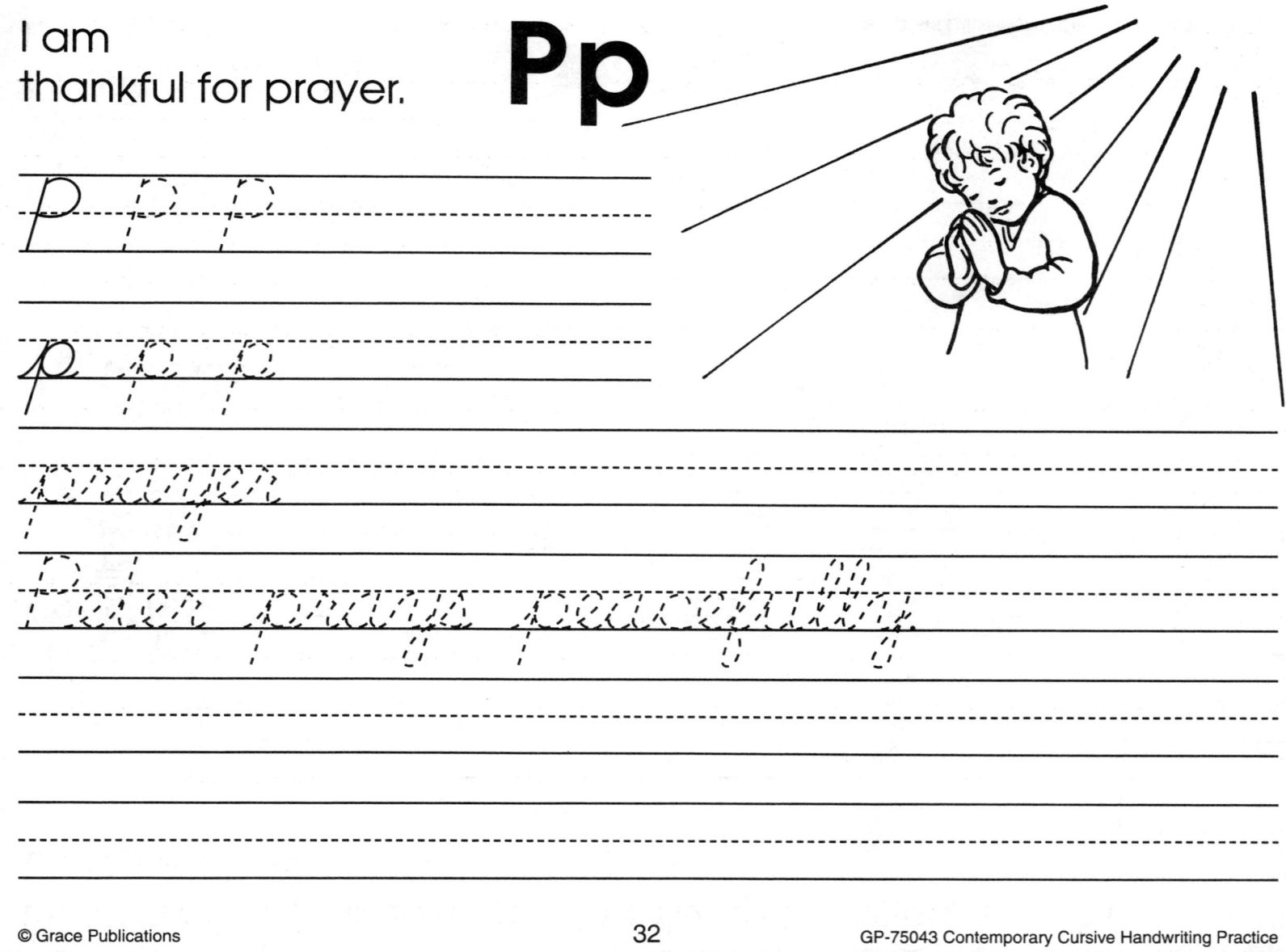

P P P

p p p

prayer

Peter prays prayerfully.

Be joyful always; pray continually; give thanks…

1 Thessalonians 5:16–18

I am thankful for quail.

Qq

Q Q Q

q q q

quail

The quail quivered.

© Grace Publications
GP-75043 Contemporary Cursive Handwriting Practice

...and he brought them quail and satisfied them with the bread of heaven.

Psalm 105:40

I am thankful for rainbows.

Rr

R R R

R R R

rainbow

I remember the rainbow.

© Grace Publications

...my rainbow...will be the sign of the covenant between me and the earth.

Genesis 9:13

Ss

I am thankful for shepherds.

…our Lord Jesus, that great Shepherd of the sheep…

Hebrews 13:20

Tt

I am thankful for trust.

Trust in the Lord and do good…

Psalm 37:3

I am thankful for understanding.

Uu

U U U

u u u

understanding

Understanding unites.

© Grace Publications   42   GP-75043 Contemporary Cursive Handwriting Practice

...a man of understanding delights in wisdom.

Proverbs 10:23

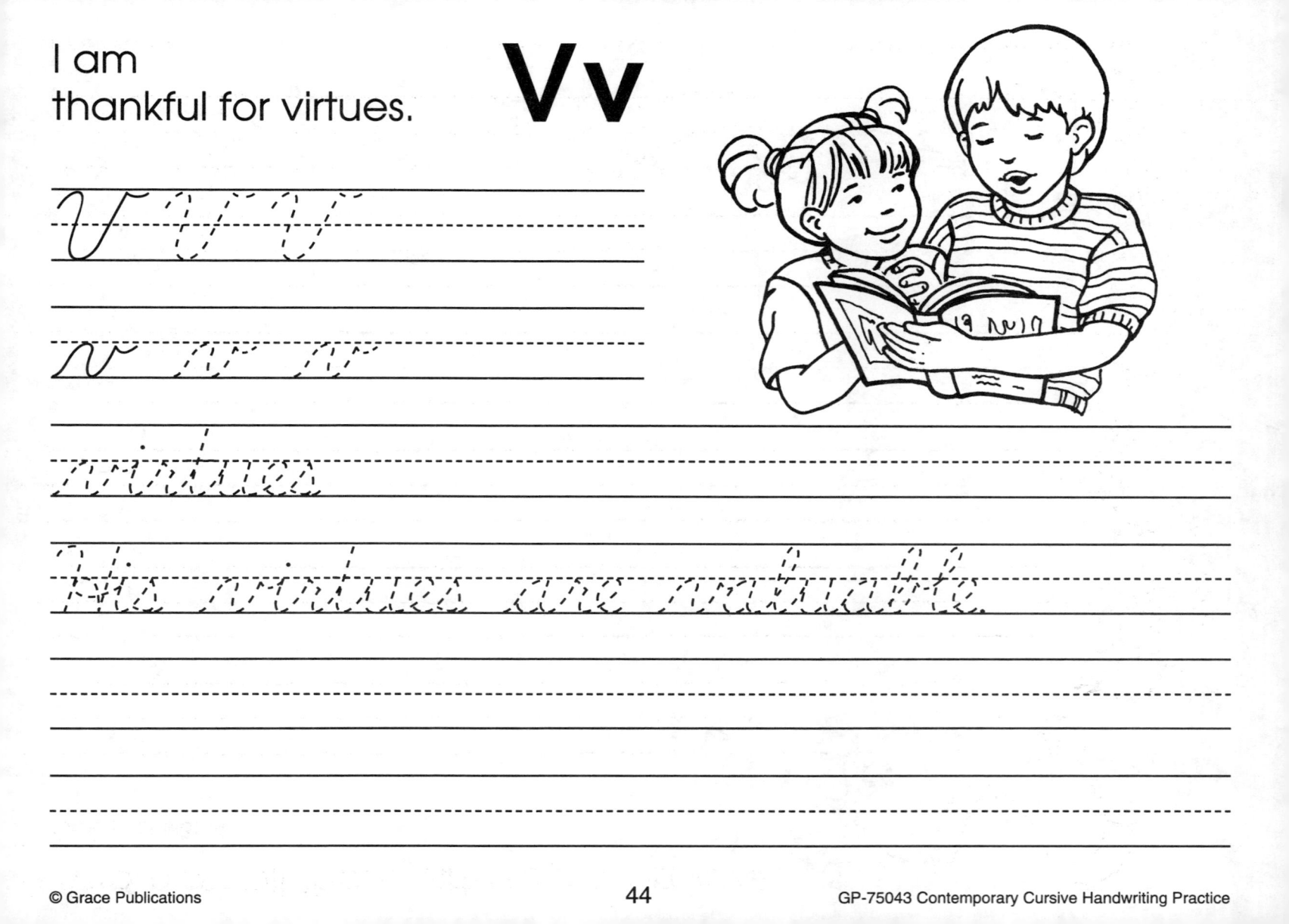

I am
thankful for virtues.

Vv

V V V

v v v

virtues

His virtues are valuable.

© Grace Publications   44   GP-75043 Contemporary Cursive Handwriting Practice

And over all these virtues put on love...

Colossians 3:14

Ww

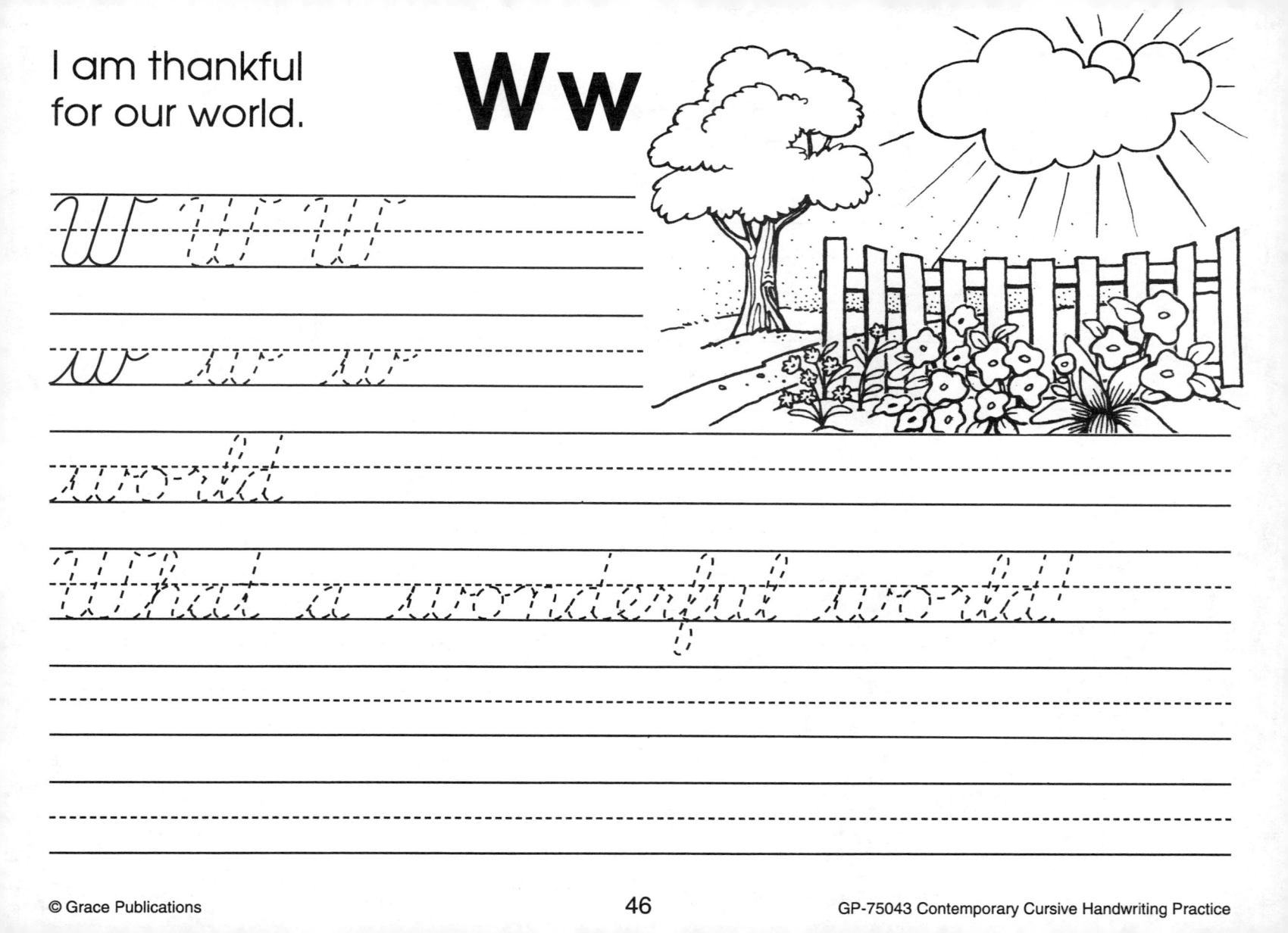

I am thankful for our world.

"...the whole world will know that there is a God..."

1 Samuel 17:46

I am thankful for King Xerxes.

Xx

$\mathcal{X}$ $\mathcal{X}$ $\mathcal{X}$

x x x

Xerxes

King Xerxes married Esther.

...Xerxes who ruled over 127 provinces stretching from India to Cush.

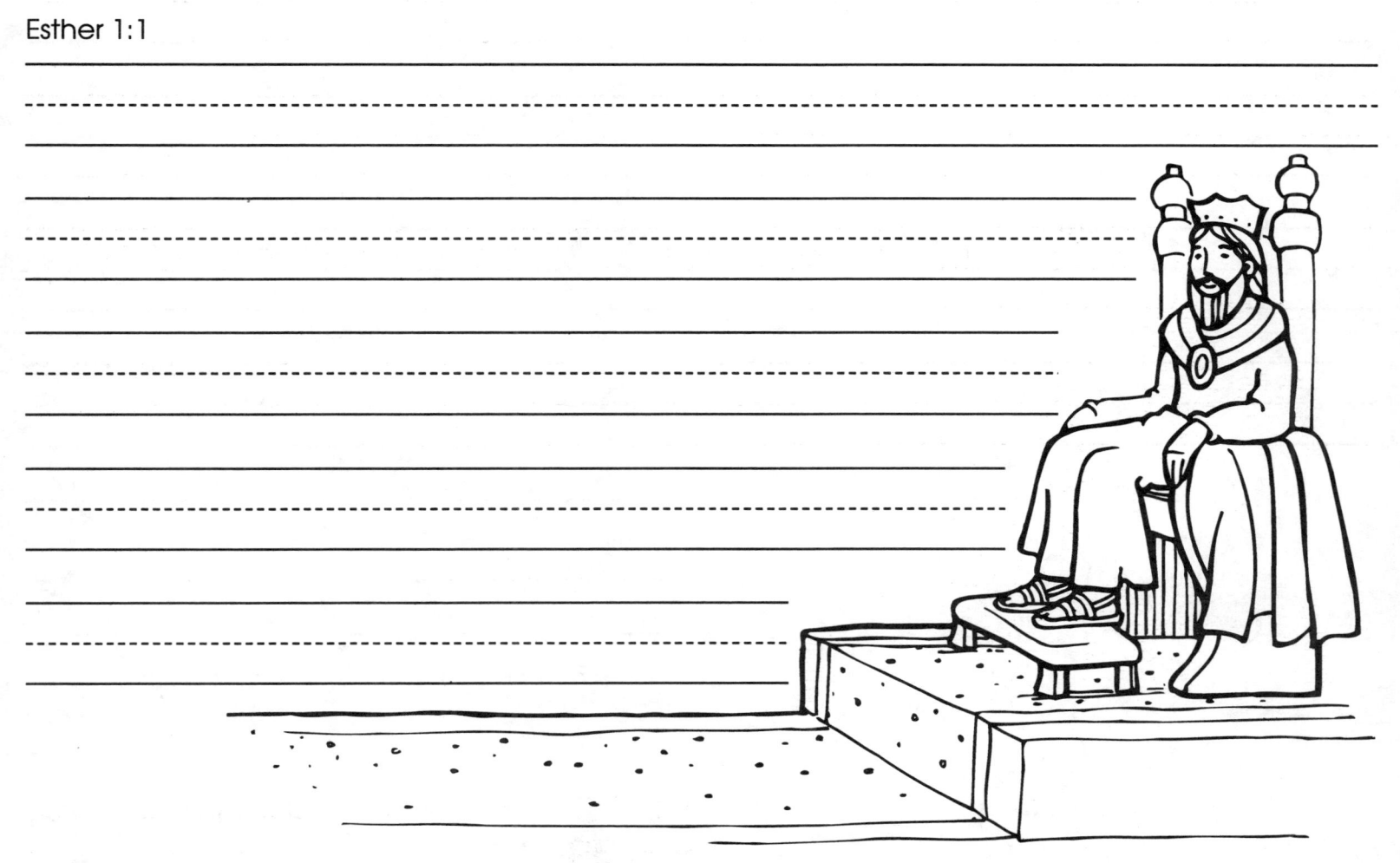

Esther 1:1

I am
thankful for my youth.

Yy

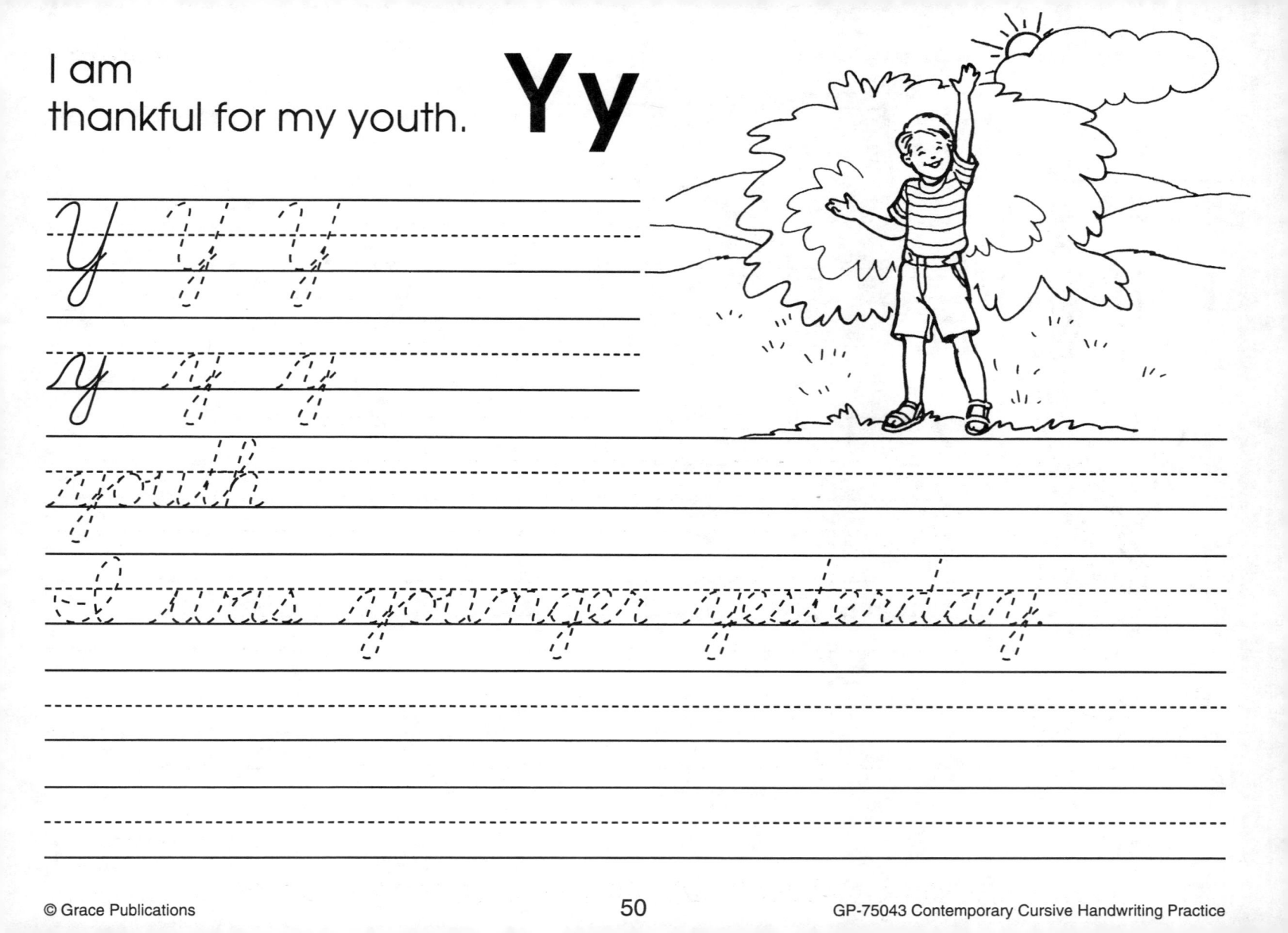

Y Y Y

y y y

youth

I am younger yesterday

© Grace Publications   50   GP-75043 Contemporary Cursive Handwriting Practice

Remember your Creator in the days of your youth...

Ecclesiastes 12:1

Zz

I am thankful for Zacchaeus.

"...Zacchaeus, come down immediately. I must stay at your house today."

Luke 19:5

Write something you are thankful for and illustrate it.

I am

thankful for

Write your favorite Bible verse below.

Congratulations!

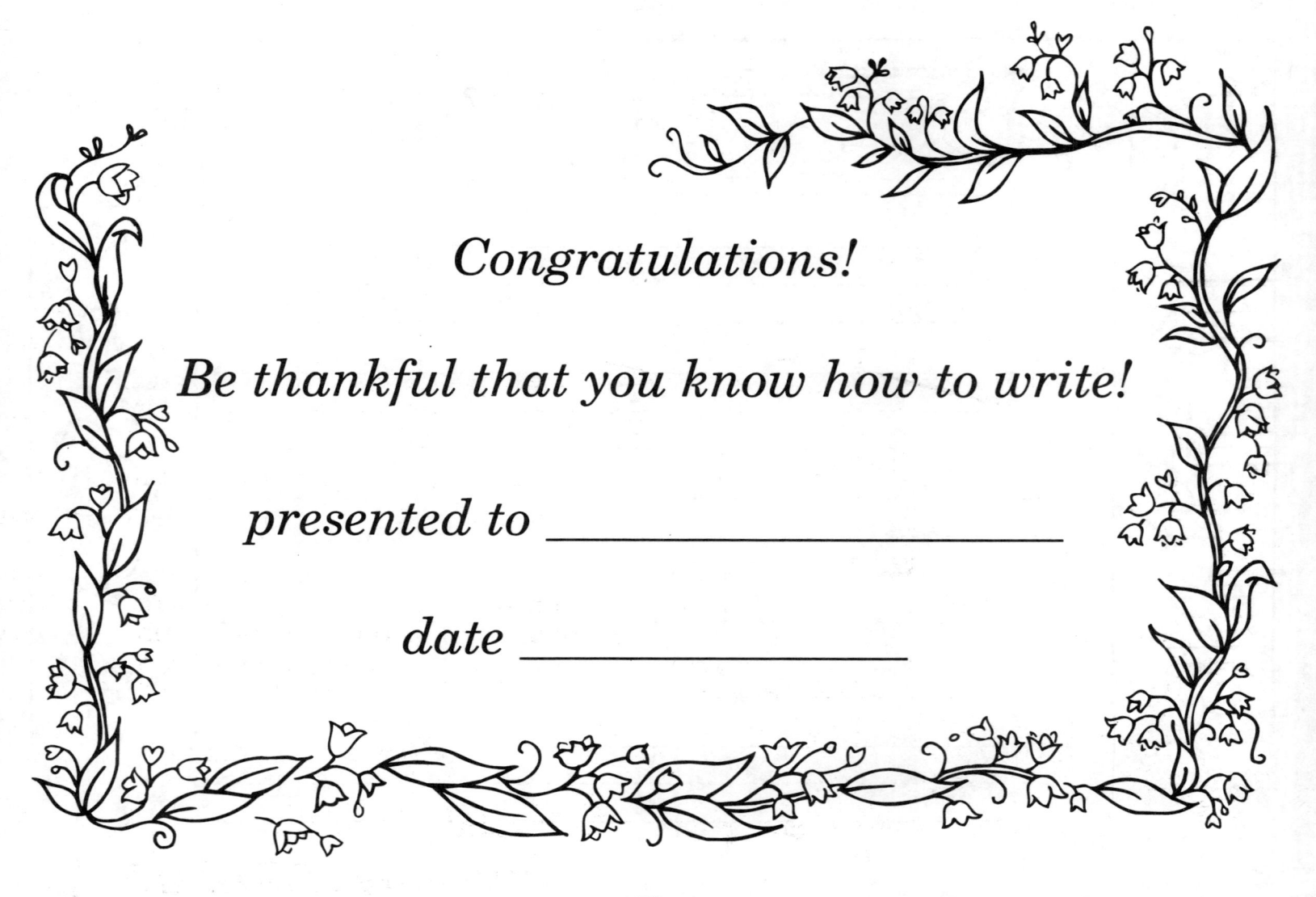

Be thankful that you know how to write!

presented to _____

date _____